AFRICA PRESENTS

THE CONGO RDC

AND

THE CONGOLESE CUISINE

FIRST EDITION

BY

BEPONA COLLECTION

AFRICA PRESENTS THE CONGO RDC AND THE CONGOLESE CUISINE

FIRST EDITION

Bepona Collection

Copyright © 2011 by Bepona Collection

ISBN: 978-0-9859230-9-9

All rights reserved. No part of this book can be reproduced or transmitted in any form by any means, electronic or mechanical, including photocopying, recording, or by any information storage and retrieval system, without the prior written permission of the publisher.

Printed in the United State of America

AFRICA

DEMOCRATIC REPUBLIC OF CONGO

KINSHASA, THE CAPITAL CITY OF THE Congo RDC PRIOR TO THE CIVIL WAR

TABLE OF CONTENT

	Page
Introduction	7
Cuisine overview	8-9
Bilolo vegetable… (Photo pge 117-118) recipe	30-31
Biteko-teko vegetable (Kalaloo) (Photo pge 119) recipe	17-20
Dongo-dongo (Okra) Photo pge 102-104) recipe	41-49
Fufu	(Photo pge 111)
Kwanga	(Photo pge 109-110)
Madesu (Beans) (Photo pge 105) recipe	65-67
Matembele vegetable (Photo pge 120) recipe	21-26
Mbisi (Fish) (Photo pge 115-116) recipe	78-79
Mfumbwa recipe	39-41
Mikate (Traditional doughnut) (Photo pge 114) recipe	87-89
Mikungu vegetable recipe	35-36
Mukiongi recipe	34
Ndji-ndji…recipes	32-33
Ngai-ngai vegetable (sour vegetable) recipe	27-30
Nkofi (Collard green) recipe	37-38
Peanut loaf (Nguba ya kotumba)	61-64
Plantain (Photo pge 112-113) recipe	83-86
Pondu vegetable (cassava leaves) (Photo pge 93-96) recipes	12-16
Poulet/Soso (Chicken) (Photo pge 121 recipes	68-74
Pumpkin Seeds (Photo pge 97-100) recipe	50-60
Viande (Meat) recipe	90-91
Yam (Photo pge 106-107) recipe	81-82

Congo RDC Cuisine

INTRODUCTION:

Many people have always asked the authors of this book: "What do the Congolese people really eat? How do the Bantu peoples cook their foods? What kind of recipes can they share with the people from the various cultures?"

Well, we are just grateful to all these inquiries, and therefore, we have decided to share some of our recipes in order to satisfy the curiosity of our friends and colleagues.

This book will illustrate vegetarian and some traditional recipes.

The recipes will appear in the following order

1. Vegetable recipes
2. Seed recipes
3. Seafood recipes – fish and shrimps,
4. Fowl recipes – Chicken
5. Duck and meat in general.

Overview of Congo RDC's Cuisine

The Congo RDC is located in the center of the African continent. The Congolese society is composed of the Bantu peoples and the Pygmies. The people speak four main Congolese languages, such as: Lingala, Kikongo ya L'Etat, Swahili, and Tshiluba. French is the Congolese national language. Basically, the names of the dishes will be translated from Lingala or Kikongo languages into English in this book.

In general people eat a variety of vegetables, but Pondu (Cassava leaves) is their major vegetable. There are several different types of vegetables, and they are cooked based on the recipe involved.

The Congolese people eat also a variety of seeds, which are also cooked according to the recipes desired. Some individuals prefer the taste of toasted seeds, whereas others prefer the taste of raw seeds (ex. pumpkin seeds).

Madeso (beans) are not toasted, but boiled under a high heat prior to adding final ingredients to finalize the cooking process.)

The Congolese people enjoy eating seafood a lot, such as fish, shrimps and baby shrimps. Further, the people like also to eat fowl (chicken and ducks). They eat meat occasionally. However, some people do not eat meat at all, by choice. Generally all the foods are organic and the taste is exquisite.

In this book we will discuss the recipes of the main dishes which we have just mentioned above. In our second edition, we will include various recipes of diverse foods.

VEGETABLE DISHES

The following are the types of vegetables the Congolese people eat regularly: Bilolo, *Biteko-Teko (Kalaloo), Dongo-Dong (okra), Matembele, Makasa ya mbika (Mubungi) – Pumpkin leaves, Mfumbwa, Mikungu, Ndji-ndji, Nkofi (collard green, Pondu (cassava leaves and spinash.*

COOKING OF VEGETABLES

Question: What is the famous vegetable dish that people always talk about and recommend tasting when you first arrive in the Congo RDC, which is the Bantu peoples' society. The answer is: *PONDU Vegetable*.

Pondu vegetable is a number one Congolese people's well known and favorite vegetable dish.

How Do Congolese People Cook Pondu?

There are two options in cooking Pondu. It all depends on the individual's taste and preference.

We will present both options.

1. Regular Pondu
2. Limbondo Pondu

Regular Pondu Recipe:

How to obtain Pondu? In the big cities and in small towns, pondu must be purchased like any other commodities. In the villages however, pondu vegetable is collected directly from cassavas fields.

See a picture of fresh pondu (cassava leaves) on the image and photos section.

Currently, the quantity or the amount requires varies with the number of people in the household or the number of guests. However, as far as the Bantu's norms are concerned, due to their hospitality towards unexpected guests, and also due to the fact that they were always used in producing a surplus, food was always cooked more than enough to spare. Nowadays, however, because of the scarcity of our modern life, we will estimate the basic measurement.

Basically, the Congolese dishes are not really depended upon any physical measurements per se; people actually have an innate sense of measurement or a common sense in cooking any type of recipe, and getting a perfect result.

Plain Regular Pondu

Ingredients

    3-5 lbs of cassava leaves

    Heavy large enough pot

    Washed cassava leaves.

    Skillet or boiled water

    Mortar/or blender

    Palm oil or Mwamba/Mossaka (palm fruit butter)

    Spices (nzete ya solo(exotic spice), hot pepper, salt, etc…).

Preparation of Regular Pondu

Soak Cassava leaves in hot water/ or pass the leaves on a very high heat skillet to ensure its softening
Wait for ten minutes in the water or/turn on skillet until soft
Remove from hot water/or from skillet
Dry out excess water prior to grinding
Grind 3-5 lbs of cassava leaves

Pour in heavy large pot

Pour 5-6 cups of water

Make sure that the pondu has been immersed completely in the water.

Add spices –salt, hot peper (green/red), salt, (an exotic spice called"Nzete ya solo" or le Mokubi Seed if available, if not replace it with any spice of your taste (even though you might not get the same exact result.

Cover the pot

Let it boil for about 60 minutes, but make sure to stir it every now and then in order to prevent burning

Add palm oil *(**attention: Palm oil is the main ingredient – because it gives pondu an authentic taste, any other type of oil cannot do it)**.*

The measurement of the oil will be dependent upon the amount of Pondu. Make sure to stir it every now and then

Use a wooden spoon to mix the content, preferably.

Let it cook for about 35 minutes.

After the pondu has turn completely golden and soft – this is an indication that the pondu has been well cooked. It must feel soft when stirring – if not -

Add some more water if need be, and let it cook.

Cover and let it boil some more until it has been well mixed with oil and water, and had turned golden and soft.

Reduce the heat and let it simmer

Turn off the burner.

Pondu can be served with rice, fufu, couscous, kwanga or plantain or yuca.

Preparation of Limbondo Pondu

Grind 3-5 lbs of cassava leaves

Pour in heavy medium or largep ot

Pour 3-4 cups of water

Make sure that the pondu has been immersed completely in the water.

Add ¼ teaspoon of baking soda

Add other ingredients sardine, or dried fish or cat fish as desired, mixed all together.

Add spices – hot pepper(green or red), salt, (an exotic spice called "nzete ya solo" or le Mokubi Seed if available to give an authentic taste, if not available, substitute it with any spice of your taste.

Cover the pot

Let it boil for about 40-45 minutes

Add ½ cup of palm oil (attention: Palm oil is the main ingredient – because it gives pondu an authentic taste, any other type of oil cannot do it).

Let it boil for about 25minutes

Use a wooden spoon to mix the content.

Do not let it burn.

After the pondu has turn completely greenish and soft – this is an indication that the pondu-Limbondo has been well cooked. Otherwise- use your discretion

Add some more water if need be – cover and let it boil

some more until it has been well mixed with oil and water

Taste it and evaluate its softness and then at that time it can be served – with the following: either: Rice, Fufu, Plantain, Kwanga or Yam.

N.B. Pondu (Limbondo) appears greenish in color

Preparation of frozen Pondu

1-3 lbs - Defrost the container
1 package of chopped spinash/1 eggplant/1 green squash
Clean it carefully with cold water
Pour it in a heavy medium cooking pot
Add spices –parboil for 45 minutes
Add spinach/ or eggplant/or green squash
Let it cook for about 25 minutes
Follow pondu or-Limbond recipe

N.B. Frozen Pondu takes sometimes a little longer to cook, and therefore use the discretion mentioned above (adding some more water to let it cook until it gets very soft).

BITEKO-TEKO (Beetako-tako) or (KALALOO) VEGETABLE

In the Congo RDC, there are three types of biteko-teko or Kalaloo vegetables:

- Long-size (2 kinds) – both grow on long stems – but one appears light-green in color, whereas another appears partially reddish.
- The short – size biteko-teko (kalaloo) vegetable grows on short stalks, and appears dark green in color.

COOKING OF BITEKO-TEKO VEGETABLE (KALALOO)

Ingredients

1-2 lbs of chopped biteko-teko (kalaloo)

1 cup of water

1 cup of chopped fresh tomatoes

1 raw hot pepper or a ¼ teaspoon of dried pepper

½ cup of peanut oil or palm oil

1/2 lbs dried/smoked boneless fish or mushroom.

Preparation

Place chopped Biteko-teko (kalaloo) in the pot

Add 1 cup of water

Let it boil for five minutes

Pour ½ cup of oil in a frying pan

Let the palm turns orange like color.

Pour chopped fresh tomatoes

Add your favorite spices including hot pepper and salt to seasoning.

Keep on stirring it until you get a homogeneous tomatoes sauce.

Add the dried fish - Let it cooked for five minutes

Pour it in the biteko-teko pot

Mixed it, and cook for about 5-6 minutes.

Remove it from the burner and

it is ready to serve with any of the following: Rice, Fufu, Plantain, Yam, Kwanga.

N.B. Biteko-teko can also be cooked plain without mixing with anything else.

For vegetarian style – Kalaloo can be mixed with mushroom of any kind, based on personal taste preference.

Preparation of short dark Biteko-teko

The majority of people prefer to steam this vegetable just like steaming spinach.

Ingredients

1-2 lbs of chopped Biteko-teko -Kalaloo)

Raw of dried pepper

1/2 cup water

2 tablespoons peanut oil

¼ teaspoon salt

1 bay leave or any spice desired.

Preparation

- ➤ Pour chopped Biteko-teko in the pot
- ➤ Add raw or dried pepper as desired
- ➤ Add ½ cup of water
- ➤ Add 2 tablespoons of peanut oil or any oil.
- ➤ Let it boil for few minutes
- ➤ Season it to taste
- ➤ Let it simmer for five minutes
- ➤ It can be served as a side dish.

MATEMBELE VEGETABLE

Matembele vegetable is cultivated. It is also a well known type of vegetable beside from Pondu vegetable. Matembele vegetable is eaten more often because of its well known composition. It appears very dark green in color.

Matembele vegetable has a variety of recipes like many other Congolese vegetables.

- Plain recipe (steam)
- Matembele with mushroom
- Matembele with smoked fish/dried fish
- Matembele with makayabo (cat fish)
- Matembele with dried shrimps of baby shrimps

Plain Matembele Recipe

Ingredients

2-3 lbs Fresh matembele
Cutting board and a sharp knife
Medium size cooking pot
1/4 cup of water
2-3 tablespoon palm oil/or peanut
Spices – Salt, hot pepper, celery, nzete ya solo or other – onion…etc.

Preparation

Wash matembele thoroughly
Peel the outer layer
Clean it for the second time
Chop it in fine layers
Place in the cooking pot
Add ¼ cup of water
Add spices
Cover it
Let it cook for 5-6 minutes

Stir it every now and then to prevent burning.
Remove from the heat
Ready to serve with either: rice, couscous, chikwanga, fufu, plaintain or Yam. ou Yuca.

Matembele Recipe with Sardine

Ingredients

2-3 lbs Fresh matembele
Cutting board and a sharp knife
Medium size cooking pot
2 cups of water
1/4 cup of palm oil/or peanut
2 ripe tomatoes
Spices – Salt, hot pepper, celery, nzete ya solo or other – onion…etc.

Preparation

Wash matembele thoroughly
Peel the outer layer
Clean it for the second time
Chop it in fine layers
Place in the cooking pot
Add 1 cup of water

Heat oil in a frying pan

Let the oil change to orange color
Add chopped tomatoes - Add spices -Cover it - Let it cook for 6 minutes

Add sardine in tomatoes sauce

Pour cooked tomatoes sauce in the pot and mix it with vegetable - Stir it every now and then to prevent burning. -Let it cook for few more minutes until cooked-Remove from the heat

Ready to serve with either: rice, couscous, chikwanga, fufu, plaintain or Yam. ou Yuca.

Matembele Recipe with Makayabo

Ingredients

2-3 lbs Fresh matembele
Cutting board and a sharp knife
Medium size cooking pot
2 cus of water
½ cup of palm oil/or peanut
1 lb of Makayabo (cat fish)
Spices – hot pepper, celery, nzete ya solo or other – onion…etc.

Preparation

Wash matembele thoroughly
Peel the outer layer
Clean it for the second time
Chop it in fine layers
Place in the cooking pot
Add 1 cup of water
Soak makayabo in cold water a night prior the cooking

Parboil makayabo for 30 minutes
Remove all the bones thoroughly
Wash it once more in cold water
Parboil vegetable for 5 minutes
Remove it from the heat
Heat oil in the frying Pan
Let it change to golden color
Add chopped tomatoes with
Add spices
Let it cooked for 5 minutes
Add boneless Makayabo, let it cook for 5 minutes.
Pour tomatoes sauce in the cooking pot
Mix it with vegetable
Cover it
Stir it every now and then to prevent burning.
Let it cook for 8 minutes until it is cooked;
Remove it from the heat
Ready to serve with either: rice, couscous, chikwanga, fufu, plaintain or Yam. ou Yuca.

NGAI – NGAI VEGETABLE

This vegetable has a wonderful aroma however it has a fresh sour taste which goes well in combination with seafood. There are three kinds of Ngai-Ngai vegetable in the Congo RDC.
The first kind is grown on the long stem. There are two categories:
1. first type has soft and reddish leaves.
2. The leaves of the second kind have two textures, light green and reddish color.

Both kinds are cultivated.

The third kinds of ngai-ngai is grown on the short stem or stalk the leaves feel kind of rough. This type of ngai-ngai grow wild in the forest, it appears green in texture, however has the same taste like the other types mentioned above.

COOKING NGAI-NGAI VEGETABLE (Sour vegetable)

There are few options in cooking ngai-ngai vegetable:

It can be cooked plain (steam), and eat it as a side dish.

It can be cooked in combination with a fresh fish.

It can be cooked in combination with a dried fish or Makayabo (cat fish)

Ngai-ngai vegetable can also be cooked in combination with Shrimps or baby shrimps or crabs.

It can be cooked with crabs.

It can be cooked with mushroom for a strict vegetarian dish.

Ingredients

2lbs Ngai-ngai vegetable
½ cup of water
Medium cooking pot
Cutting board and knife
Cooking instructions - Plain ngai-ngai

1. Remove the leaves from the stems
2. Clean it well to remove the dus
3. 1-2 lbs of ngai-ngai
4. Pour ½ of water
5. Bring it to boil
6. Add 2-3 tablespoons or any oil of your choice
7. Add spices of your choice
8. Season to taste
9. Simmer and serve with (fufu, kwanga or Yam)

Ngai-Ngai with Fresh Fish or Shrimps

1. Remove the leaves from the stems
2. Clean it well to remove the dust
3. 1-2 lbs of chopped ngai-ngai
4. Pour in the cooking pot
5. Pour 1 ½ cup of water
6. Bring it to boil for 5 minutes
7. Cut the fish into normal size
8. Chopped fresh tomatoes
9. Sauté fresh fish or shrimps- in palm oil.

10. Sauté chopped fresh tomatoes- in palm oil
11. Add spices of your choice - salt
12. Mixed fried fish, in tomatoes sauce –Cover it
13. Let it cook for about 10 minutes

Season to taste and serve with either fufu or plantain, kwanga, and couscous.

BILOLO VEGETABLE *tastes as broccoli rabe)*

There are two types of bilolo vegetable in the Congo RDC. One type has a wide leaves and the kind has thin leaves. Both appear dark green color, in fact they are darker than any other known green.

Bilolo can be cooked in different varieties

It can be steam (plain) adding 1 or 2 tablespoons palm oil.

It could be cooked mixed with dried fish, or with makayabo (cat fish.)

Bilolo vegetable taste better when cooked in palm paste or butter (called Mwamba –mbila or mwamba ya nguba (peanut butter).

Cooking Bilolo Vegetable

Ingredients

1 lb of chopped bilolo vegetable 1 cup water chopped fresh tomatoes

1 whole or chopped raw pepper or ¼ of dried hot pepper.

½ cup of palm oil or peanut oil

2 cups of Mwamba –mbila sauce or 3 tablespoons peanut butter

1 bay leave or –1 piece of Nzete ya solo/mokubi or ¼ tiny piece of mukubi fruit (Congolese spice).

What is - NDJI-NDJI VEGETABLE

The ndji-ndji vegetale is originated from a special type of Yam found usually in Bandundu region. This type of vegetable tastes similar to ASPARAGUS, however, ndji-ndji can grow up from o few inches to one foot tall. This type of yam is not cultivated, it grows wild in the forest, and it is a seasonal vegetable.

This vegetable is very easy to cook. Usually it is steamed in order to conserve its texture. It can also be mixed with different type of vegetable, such as Mubungi (makasa ya mbika – pumpkin seeds's leaves) in some of regions of the country.

Ingredient

1-2 lbs of of clean Ndji-ndji

Cut ndji-ndji depending in its size (two, tree or four pieces)

1-2 tablespoons palm oil

½ cup of water

1 raw green hot pepper

Preparation of Ndji-Ndji Vegetable

- *Place the stuck of cut ndji-ndji in a medium pot*
- *pour ½ cup of water*
- *Add 1 raw green hot pepper*
- *Add 1-2 tablespoons of palm oil*
- *Add salt to seasoning*
- *Cover it*
- *Boil it for about 4-6 minutes*
- *Stir it until it becomes soft.*
- *Serve it as a side dish.*

When Ndji-ndji is mixed with other vegetable and Makayabo (cat fish) or dried chunk fish can be served as a main dish. with rice, fufu, plantain, couscous or Yam.

MUKIONGI VEGETABLE (MISILI)

MISILI or Mukiongi can be classified in the Ndji-ndji category. It grows wild in the forest.

How to cook Misili?

Misili as Ndji-ndji are long vegetable. It can grow up to ½ a foot.

Usely it is sold per a bunch just like Asparagus.

Clean Misili in cold water
Cut into small pieces 1-2 pounds
Pour the pieces into a medium cooking pot
Add 2 ½ cup of water
Add baby shrimps or big shrimps as desired.
Add 1 raw green-hot pepper or ¼ teaspoon dried hot pepper

Add 2-3 tablespoons of palm oil or peanut oil

Add salt and any preferred spices to give it more flavors.
Cover and cook for about 20 minutes
Taste it and serve with either – fufu, rice, couscous, plantain, Kwanga or Yam.

MIKUNGU VEGETABLE

This is another type of vegetable that grows wild in the forest. It tastes very crunch. It is white color inside. It has such an exceptional aroma.

Mikungu is enveloped in its special long shell or a jacket. It can grow up to one foot just like Ndji-ndji does.

People have a special way of pulling mikungu from the ground. Mikungu are sold in bunch just like ndji-ndji.

Mikungu shells must be open meticulously in order to bring the whole thing out of the shell; otherwise it would break into pieces, which is not so good in terms of marketing activity.

THE PREPARATION OF MIKUNGU VEGETABLE

- *Break the shell open*
- *Pull the white substance out of the shell*
- *Clean them with the cold water*
- *It all depends on the length of each mikungu*
- *Cut them into medium size*
- *Place them in a medium size Pot, or in a large pot according to the amount of mikungu.*
- *if 1-2 lbs, add ½ lb cup of water*
- *Add 1-2 tablespoons of palm oil or peanut oil*
- *Add spice – hot pepper (green or red)*

Cover it and let it boil or steam it until it gets soft and ready to serve

Mikungu vegetable can be mixed with other type of vegetables to give a special aroma.
In order to obtain an authentic taste, all these vegetable should be cooked in a palm oil or mwamba-mbila (palm fruit paste)- Mikungu vegetable can be cooked in combination with dried fish, baby shrimp, mushroom, or Makayabo.

*N.B. **The following vegetables: Ndji-ndji, Misili (Mokiongi), Mikungu, Mubungi (Pumpkin Seed), most of them are originating from Bandundu Province.***

NKOFI (Collar Green)

This vegetable is cultivated in the Congo RDC.

It can be cooked also in different ways. It is always cooked in palm fruit sauce, or in peanut butter sauce) in order to reach an authentic taste.

Vegetarian style

Nkofi or collar green is cooked usually with mushroom. Traditional style – Nkofi is cooked in combination with either of dried fish or Makayabo.

Ingredient

- *Chopped nkofi*
- *Dried fish, or Makayabo, or mushroom,*
- *Raw or dried hot pepper*
- *Palm fruit sauce (mwamba-mbila) or mwamba-nguba (peanut butter sauce)*
- *Spices (depends on personal taste or preference)*

Preparation of Nkofi (collar green)

- *1-2 lbs of chopped Nkofi green (finely)*
- *Place the chopped collar green in a medium cooking pot*
- *Add 1-3 cups palm fruit sauce or 1-2 cups of peanut butter sauce.*
- *Can add canned tomatoes sauce if so desired or* **you can completely omit tomatoes sauce in this recipe.**
- *Add either – Mushroom or dried fish, or Makayabo(n.b.cat fish must be soaked in the cold water, and then boil under high heat for about 10 minutes in order to remove excess salt.*
- *Make sure to remove all the bones prior to mixing it with the vegetable.*
- *Add spices – raw, or dried hot pepper aromatic nut (nzete ya solo*
- *Cover the pot*
- *Let it cook under high temperature for about 25 minutes.*
- *Reduce the heat, stirring it often*
- *Remove it from the heat*
- *Ready to be served with whatever starch of your choice.*

MFUMBWA (uhm-fum-boua) Vegetable

Mfumbwa is not cultivated because it grows wild in the Congo RDC's forest.

How the Congolese ancestors knew that this leave was edible?

Answer: They were just inspired by God that such leave was safe and fit for human consumption.

Mfumbwa vegetable is consumed more in one part of the country than in the rest of the country. However Pondu vegetable is eaten throughout the country. It is the country's main vegetable dish.

Bear in mind however that peanut butter is the main ingredient in the cooking of Mfumbwa vegetable. No one can do without it. However, in terms of combination – Mfumbwa can be cooked with smoked fish, with sardine or with Makayabo.

Ingredients

2 lbs of mfumbwa

1/2 cup of peanut

3-4 cup of water

a cutting board

1 cup of small pieces of smoked fish

2 or 3 ripe fresh tomatoes

Spice (cayenne, salt, nzete ya solo (onion or any other spices)

Preparation

- Wash Mfumbwa leaves throughouly
- Use a cutting board and sharp knife
- Cut mfumbwa very fine
- Place the chopped mfumbwa in the medium cooking Pot
- Dissolve ½ cup of peanut butter

- *Add 3 cups of water based on the amount of mfumbwa*
- *Add the fresh chopped tomatoes and spices*
- *Cover the pot*
- *Let it cook under high heat for about 35 minutes*
- *Make sure to stir it constantly to prevent burning.*
- *Reduce the heat and simmer for awhile*
- *Then remove it from the heat ready to serve.- either*
- **with –, Chikwanga, Couscous Fufu, Plantain, Rice, or Yam,**

DONGO-DONGO(Gombo) OKRA

Okra can be cooked plain or in combination with seafood or with mushroom. Basically, in the Congo RDC people eat fresh vegetables.

The following is the listing of Okra recipes

Plain Okra must yield green color

Okra with mushroom

Okra with raw fish

Okra with shrimps

Okra with baby shrimps

Okra with dried or smoked fish

Okra with Makayabo (cat fish)

Recommended spices are the following:

Raw basil leave, bay leave, Nzete ya solo (mukubi fruit)

or can be replaced with any of your favorite spices (onion, or..)

Plain Okras Dish

Iingredients

1-2lbs fresh okra

Cutting board and sharp knife

Raw green or red pepper

2 cups of cold water

¼ teaspoon baking soda

Fresh basil (2 leaves)

Nzete ya solo (Mukubi fruit) if available or any other spice

1-3 tablespoons of palm oil or can be substituted

Preparation of plain okra

- *Clean fresh okras in cold water*
- *Chopped regular size*
- *Place chopped okra in a medium size pot*
- *Add 2 cups of cold water*
- *Add ¼ teaspoon baking soda (*
- *Add 1 raw whole or chopped hot pepper*
- *Add 1-3 tablespoons of palm oil or any other type*
- *Add all the necessary spices and salt-*
- *Cover the pot*
- *Parboil okra*
- *Let it cooked under high heat for about 20 minutes*
- *Reduce the heat, let it simmer*
- *Remove from the heat*

*Ready to serve –***with either one of the following: fufu, chikwanga, plaintain, Yam**

Okra dish with smoked fish

Ingredients

1-2lbs fresh okra

Cutting board and sharp knife

2 ripe tomatoes

Raw green or red pepper

2 cups of cold water

1 cup of dried fish pieces

½ cup of palm oil

Fresh basil (2 leaves), 1 bay leave

Nzete ya solo (Mukubi fruit) if available or any other spice Salt

Preparation of Okra with Dried or SMOKED FISH

- *Clean fresh okras in cold water*
- *Chopped regular size*
- *Place chopped okra in a medium size pto*
- *Soak dried or smoked fish in cold water*
- *Remove all the bones*
- *Add 2 cups of cold water*
- *Add 1 raw green/red whole or chopped hot pepper*
- *A Cover the pot*
- *Parboil okra for 10 minutes*
- *Heat 1/2 cup of palm oil/or any available in the frying pan*
- *Pour chopped tomatoes and cooked for 5 minutes*
- *Add all the necessary spices and salt-*
- *Add smoked fish*
- *Let it cooked under high heat for about 20 minutes*
- *Keep on stirring it to prevent burning*
- *Reduce the heat, let it simmer*
- *Remove from the heat – and ready to serve –* **with either one of the following: fufu, chikwanga, plaintain, yam**

Ingredients

1-2lbs fresh okra

Cutting board and sharp knife

2 ripe tomatoes

Raw green or red pepper

2 cups of cold water

1 cup of Makayabo pieces

½ cup of palm oil

Fresh basil (2 leaves), 1 bay leave, hot pepper, salt

Nzete ya solo (Mukubi fruit) if available or use any other spice

Preparation of okra dish with Makayabo (cat fish)

- *Clean fresh okras in cold water*
- *Chopped okra in small size*
- *Place chopped okra in a medium size pot*
- *Add 2 cups of cold water*
- *Soak Makayabo (cat fish) in cold water*

- Parboil it for 15 minutes to remove excess salt
- Remove all the bones
- Parboil okra for 10 minutes
- Add 1 raw green/red whole or chopped hot pepper
- A Cover the pot
- Heat 1/2 cup of palm oil/or any available in the frying pan
- Pour chopped tomatoes in the frying pan and cook it for 5 minutes
- Add all the necessary spices and salt-
- Add makayabo
- Let it cooked under high heat for about 20 minutes
- Keep on stirring it to prevent burning
- Reduce the heat, let it simmer
- Remove from the heat -Ready to serve

OKRA WITH FRESH FISH/SHRIMP/CRAB

Ingredients

1-2lbs fresh okra

Cutting board and sharp knife

2 ripe tomatoes

Raw green or red pepper

2 cups of cold water

2-4 pieces of fresh fish

1cup of palm oil

Fresh basil (2 leaves), 1 bay leave

Nzete ya solo (Mukubi fruit) if available or any other spice

<u>Preparation of Okra Dish with a Fresh Fish</u>

- *Clean fresh okras in cold water*
- *Chopped okra in small size*
- *Place chopped okra in a medium size pot*
- *Add 2 cups of cold water*
- *Clean the fish thoroughly*
- *Cut it into regular size*
- *Season with salt and hot pepper*
- *Parboil okra for 10 minutes*
- *Add 1 raw green/red whole or chopped hot pepper*
- *A Cover the pot*
- *Heat 1 cup of palm oil/or any available in the frying pan*
- *Fry fish slightly and remove it from the frying pan*

- *Heat fresh oil in the frying pan*
- *Pour chopped fresh tomatoes mixed with spice for 5 minutes*
- *Add fried fish-Cover the pot*
- *Let it cooked under medium heat for about 20 minutes*
- *Keep on stirring it to prevent burning*
- *Reduce the heat, let it simmer*
- *Remove from the heat*
- *Ready to serve*

N.B. **Follow the same recipes for Shrimp and Mushroom**

SEEDS RECIPES

CONGO RDC/BANTU STYLE

The Congo RDC produces different kinds of Seeds-such as: Corn, Peanut, and the famous PUMPKIN SEED. Pumpkin seed are classified in two categories:They can be distinguished from the appearance of their shells. Some pumpkin seed has golden fragile shell which can be broken easily with a fingertip.

They appear white inside. Other types of pumpkin seed however have white shells which seem harsh and stiff.

They are therefore hard to break with a fingertip. They necessitate the use of other means to have it broken. This type of pumpkin seed appears green inside.

PUMPKIN SEED IS A WELL KNOWN SEED IN THE CONGO RDC which is the society of Bantu Peoples and the Pygmies. In the seed section, we will see how to cook the varieties of pumpkin seed recipes.

Everyone practically in the Congo RDC eats pumpkin seedsDepending on different Areas – It is called either Mbika, Ntere and Mantete.

There are 4 different recipes with pumpkin seeds:

1. *Pumpkin seed with Mushroom*
2. *Pumpkin seed with Fresh/fried fish*
3. *Pumpkin seed with dried/smoked fish or Makayabo*
4. *Pumpkin seed with fresh Shrimps or baby shrimps*
5. *Pumpkin seed dish with Mushroom*
6. *Pumpkin with chicken*

Baked pumpkin seed must always be mixed with other ingredients. Bear in mind however that the main spice that gives an exotic flavor in pumpkin seed is FRESH BASIL.

N.B. Pumpkin seed cannot be cooked plain, it should always be mixed with other ingredients for a best result.

COOKING PUMPKIN SEEDS

Pumpkin seed with Mushroom

Ingredients
- 1-2 lbs of pumpkin seed without shell
- Frying pan
- Traditional mortar or a blender
- Medium cooking pot
- Mushroom
- Green pepper
- Green or red hot pepper
- Water
- ½ cup palm oil or any type as desired
- Fresh basil –can add any spice desired.
- Salt

PREPARATION OF PUMPKIN SEED WITH MUSHROOM

- 2-4 lbs pumpkin seed
- Wash the seeds in order to remove dust
- Place the frying pan on the heat
- Toast the seed lightly
- Pour one cup of water in the blender to grind it

if the mortar is not available. – make sure to get a homogeneous paste without any granule
Pour one cup of cold water in the pot
Bring it to boil
Pour the paste in the boiling water slowly
Parboil it
Chopped 2 ripe tomatoes
Clean mushroom and slice it
Heat ¼ cup of palm oil on the frying pan
Pour chopped tomatoes in the pan
Pour chopped basil and salt
Add mushroom in the pot mixed slightly cover the pot and let it cook for 10 minutes until it is cooked

Ready to serve with eith Fufu, chikwanga (kwanga), plantain, couscous or Yam..

Chicken in pumpkin seeds sauce

Ingredients

1-2 lbs of pumpkin seed without shell
Frying pan
Traditional mortar or a blender
Medium cooking pot
Chicken 5-8 pieces
3 ripe tomatoes
Green or red hot pepper
Water
1 cup palm oil or any type as desired
Fresh basil –can add any spice desired.
Salt

PREPARATION

1-4 lbs pumpkin seed
Wash the seeds in order to remove dust
Place the frying pan on the heat
Toast the seed lightly or grind it raw

Pour one cup of water in the blender to grind it if the mortar is not available. – make sure to get a homogeneous paste without any granule

Place chicken in heavy large enough pot

Pour 4 cups of water

Add salt and pepper

Parboil it

Dissolve pumpkin seed in the water

Add the sauce in the pot

Heat ½ cup of palm oil in the frying pan

Sauter chopped tomatoes mixed with spices

Let is cooked for 5 minutes and pour it in the pot

Let it cook for 40 minutes.

Reduce the heat

Remove the pot from the heat and ready to serve.

With Fufu, chikwanga(kwanga), plantain, couscous or Yam..

PUMPKIN SEEDS RECIPES

Ingredients

1-2 lbs of pumpkin seed without shell

Frying pan

Traditional mortar or a blender

Medium cooking pot

Chicken 5-8 pieces/or substitute with Fish

3 ripe tomatoes

Green or red hot pepper-Water

1 cup palm oil or any type as desired

Fresh basil –can add any spice desire, hot pepper, salt

PREPARATION OF PUMPKIN SEED With Fried Fish

- *1-4 lbs pumpkin seed*
- *Wash the seeds in order to remove dust*
- *Place the frying pan on the heat*
- *Toast the seed for 2 minutes/ or grind it raw*
- *Pour one cup of water in the blender to grind it, if the mortar is not available. – make sure to get a homogeneous paste without any granule at the end.*
- *Clean fish thoroughly*
- *Cut it into medium sizes*
- *On the frying pan pour 1 cup of palm/peanut oil*
- *Season fish with cayenne pepper, basil, salt or any other preferred spices*
  Sauté fish slightly
- *Add chopped fresh tomatoes*
- *Let it cook for 5 minutes*
- *Remove from the frying pan and place it in a medium cooking pot.*
- *Dissolve pumpkin seed in 1cup of water*
- *Add pumpkin sauce in the pot*

- *Add ½ cup of water*
- *Let it cooked for 8 minutes*
- *Reduce the heat let is simmer*
- *Remove it from the heat.*

Ready to serve with any of the following: Fufu, chikwanga(kwanga), plantain, couscous or Yam..

BAKED PUMPKIN SEED with baby shrimps

Ingredients

1-2 lbs of pumpkin seed without shell
Frying pan
Traditional mortar or a blender
Mixing bowl
Zombi leaves or a saucepan
1lb of baby shrimps
Green or red hot pepper
1 cup of water
Fresh basil –can add any spice desired.
Salt

Preparation

1-2 lbs pumpkin seed

Wash the seeds in order to remove dust

Place the frying pan on the heat

Toast the seed for 2 minutes/ or grind it rawPour one cup of water in the blender to grind it, if the mortar is not available. – make sure to get a homogeneous paste without any granule at the end

Pour pumpkin seed dough in the mixing bowl.

Clean baby shrimpsthoroughly

On the frying pan pour 1/4 cup of palm or peanut oil

Season baby shrimps with hot pepper, basil, salt or any other preferred spices

Sauté baby shrimps for 1 minute

Mix fried baby shrimps with pumpkin seed dough.

Wrap one portion of the dough traditionally it is done on special leaves called Nzombi leaves (makasa ya kwanga). Part each portion of the dough, about ¼, wrap it on two leaves in order to secure the content, and thrn bake it. However if zombie leaves are not available, the entire dough can be spread over a large enough pan and bake it for 30 minutes

Removed from the oven and should be ready to serve.

It can be served hot or cold.

Ready to serve with any of the following: Fufu, chikwanga (kwanga), plantain, couscous or Yam..

PEANUT BUTTER LOAF

We have four different recipes of peanut butter loaf

Peanut butter loaf with Mushroom

Peanut butter loaf with dried/smoked fish

Peanut butter loaf with Makayabo (cat fish)

Peanut butter loaf with Shrimps or baby shrimps

Ingredients
Homemade peanut butter

2-3 lbs dried peanuts

Saucepan to roast peanuts with our without shells

Remove shells

Grind roasted peanut in the Mortar

Spread enough peanut butter on the cutting board

Crush granulated peanut butter until it becomes smooth

Peanut Butter Loaf with Mushroom

Ingredient

Mixing bowl

1-2 lbs smooth peanut butter

½ cup of water

1lb of sliced mushroom

1 Green pepper

Spices- based on individual taste or preference

Preparation

- *Place peanut butter in the mixing bowl*
- *Add ½ cup water*
- *Mix sliced mushroom with peanut but thoroughly*
- *Chopped green pepper*
- *Mix chopped green together with peanut butter*
- *Add spices desired*
- *Use traditional leaves to wrap 3 or five loaf/or*
- *Bake the dough in the saucepan for 15-20 minutes*
- *Remove from the heat or the oven*
- *Ready to serve as a side dish*

Peanut Butter Loaf with Shrimps or baby shrimps

Ingredient

Mixing bowl

1-2 lbs smooth peanut butter

½ cup of water

½ baby shrimps or shrimps

1 Green pepper

Spices- celery, cayenne salt (onion, etc..)

Preparation

- Place peanut butter in the mixing bowl
- Add ½ cup water
- Clean baby shrimps well
- Mix them with peanut butter dough
- Chop green pepper
- Add in the peanut butter
- Add spices preferred

- *Use traditional leaves to wrap 3 or five loaves/or*
- *Bake the dough in the saucepan for 15-20 minutes*
- *Remove from the heat/oven*
- *Ready to serve as a side dish*

N.B. Recipes of peanut butter loaf with Dried fish is similar with the above recipes – Just substitute shrimps by dried or boneless fish or makayabo.

Corn is cooked in different recipes

Corn meal is always mixed with cassava flour in order to make Fufu. Good nutritious fufu should appear golden, this is an indication that fufu was made from ½ and 1/2 of each flour, that is corn and cassava four.

Corn on the cab and boil fresh peanut is a well know traditional snack in the Congo RDC or in the Bantu society.

MADESU (BEANS)

The Congo RDC is a society of Bantu peoples and the Pygmies. Bantu people cultivate the following types of Madesu (Beans): Madesu ya ba soda (kidney beans), Madesu ya bembe (Northern white beans) and Mbwengi (black eye peas).

There are various Beans recipes

1. *Madesu ya pamba (Plain Beans*
2. *Madesu na mbisi ya ko kwuka (Beans with dried fish*
3. *Madesu na Makayabo (beans with cat fish)*

Plain beans - Madesu ya pamba recipe

Ingredients

1-2 lbs of madesu (beans)

1 pt of water

A heavy medium cooking pot

½ cup palm oil/peanut oil

2 ripes tomatoes chopped

Spices : bay leave, celery, hot pepper, salt, or onion

Preparation

- ❖ Wash beans
- ❖ Place beans in a large cooking pot
- ❖ Add 1 pt of water
- ❖ Soak beans overnight in the water
- ❖ Parboil it under a high heat until it is soft

Pour ½ cup of palm oil in a frying pan

Heat it until it turns orange

Pour chopped fresh tomatoes

Add all spices and keep on stirring it until cooked

Pour tomatoes sauce on Madesu (beans)'s pot

Cover it and let it cook under medium heat for 1 hour. Make sure to stir it every now and then in order to prevent burning.

Reduce the heat; let it simmer for a while

Remove from the heat- and ready to serve either with rice, couscous, kwanga, plantain or yam.

FOWL RECIPES

The Bantu society of the Congo RDC has three main chicken recipes in general.

1. Poulet à la Mwamba (chicken in peanut butter sauce) -Poulet cooked in palm oil/or peanut oil.
2. Poulet cooked in tomatoes sauce)/ or fried
3. Chicken in pumpkin sauce

Spices in these recipes vary with individual taste: Bay leave, celery, cayenne, salt, (onion, or other types of spices).

POULET/Fowl GRILLER (Fried) RECIPE

Ingredients

8-10 pieces of chicken

Frying Pan

4 cups palm oil

Spices – Salt, bay leave, celery, hot pepper (or onion, etc)

PREPARATION

- *Clean chicken*

- *Season it*

- *Parboil for about 1 hour*

- *Remove from the heat*

- *Heat palm oil in a frying pan*

- *Wait until the oil turns orange color*

- *Deep fry chicken until it is cooked*

- *Remove from the frying pan*

- *Wait until it turns golden*

- *Remove from the heat*

Ready to serve- With either rice, chikwangue, plantain, fufu, couscous, Sweet potatoes or Yam.

POULET/Fowl A la Mwamba

RECIPE – chicken cooked in Peanut butter sauce.

Ingredients

8-10 pieces of chicken

½ cup of peanut butter

½ cup of palm oil

5cups of water

3 medium ripe tomatoes

1/2 canned tomatoes

Spices – Bay leave, celery, hot pepper (or onion, etc.

PREPARATION

- *Clean chicken*
- *Put in a heavy cooking pot*
- *Season it*
- *Parboil for about 1 hour*
- *Remove from the heat*
- *Heat palm oil in a frying pan*
- *Wait until the oil turns orange color*
- *Fry chicken until it turns golden*
- *Remove from the frying pan*
- *Place it in a heavy cooking pot*
- *Add the remaining water from the initial pot*
- *Heat new fresh oil in a frying pan*
- *Wait until it turns golden*
- *Add chopped tomatoes and ½ canned tomatoes*
- *Let it cook until for 5 minutes*
- *Pour in the pot*

- *Dissolve ½ of peanut butter in the water*
- *Pour it in the pot and mix it with the meat*
- *Cover it and let it cook for 35 minutes*
- *Use your discretion if the chicken is not well cooked*
- *Add some more water-*
- *Let it cook for about ten more minutes*
- *Reduce the heat and let it simmer*
- *Remove from the heat*

Ready to serve- With either, rice, chikwangue, plantain, fufu, couscous, Sweet potatoes or Yam.

POULET/Fowl in Pumpkin Seed Sauce

RECIPE – chicken cooked in Pumpkin Seed Sauce.

Ingredients

8-10 pieces of chicken

½ cup of Pumpkin paste

½ cup of palm oil

5cups of water

3 medium ripe tomatoes

1/2 canned tomatoes

Spices – Bay leave, celery, hot pepper (or onion, *etc.*

PREPARATION

- *Clean chicken*
- *Put in a heavy cooking pot*
- *Season it*
- *Parboil for about 1 hour*
- *Remove from the heat*
- *Heat palm oil in a frying pan*
- *Wait until the oil turns orange color*
- *Fry chicken until it turns golden*
- *Remove from the frying pan*
- *Place it in a heavy cooking pot*
- *Add the remaining water from the initial pot*
- *Heat new fresh oil in a frying pan*

- *Wait until it turns golden*
- *Add chopped tomatoes and ½ canned tomatoes*
- *Let it cook until for 5 minutes*
- *Pour in the pot*
- *Dissolve ½ of pumpkin paste in the water*
- *Pour it in the pot and mix it with the meat*
- *Cover it and let it cook for 35 minutes*
- *Use your discretion if the chicken is not well cooked*
- *Add some more water-*
- *Let it cook for about ten more minutes*
- *Reduce the heat and let it simmer*
- *Remove from the heat*

Ready to serve- With either, rice, chikwangue, plantain, fufu, couscous, Sweet potatoes or Yam.

DUCK RECIPES (Fresh

Ingredients

6-8 pieces of duct

½ cup of palm oil

5cups of water

3 medium ripe tomatoes

1/2 canned tomatoes

Spices – Bay leave, celery, hot pepper (or onion, etc.

PREPARATION

- *Clean duck*
- *Put in a heavy cooking pot*
- *Season it*
- *Parboil for about 1 hour*
- *Remove from the heat*
- *Heat palm oil in a frying pan*
- *Wait until the oil turns orange color*

- *Fry duck until it turns golden*
- *Remove from the frying pan*
- *Place it in a heavy cooking pot*
- *Add the remaining water from the initial pot*
- *Heat new fresh oil in a frying pan*
- *Wait until it turns golden*
- *Add chopped tomatoes and ½ canned tomatoes*
- *Let it cook until for 5 minutes*
- *Pour in the pot*
- *Cover it and let it cook for 35 minutes*
- *Use your discretion if the duck is not well cooked*
- *Add some more water-*
- *Let it cook for about fifteen minutes*
- *Reduce the heat and let it simmer*
- *Remove from the heat*

Ready to serve- With either, rice, chikwangue, plantain, fufu, couscous, Sweet potatoes or Yam.

FRIED FOODS RECIPES

PLANTAIN

YAM

Sweet Yuca

MIKATE

FISH

CHICKEN

MBISI YA KOKALINGA - FRIED FISH

The Congolese waters are known to have varieties of fishes.

The taste of Congolese fishes is very different from the taste of the fish in many other countries. The taste is known to be excellent. Probably this is due to the types of waters that those fishes grow in.

Ingredients

6-8 pieces of fish

Frying pan

2 cups of palm oil

Cutting board and sharp knife

Spices (cayenne, salt, celery, nzete ya solo, or add your favorite spice – onion etc....)

PREPARATION

- Wash fish thoroughly

- Season it with all your favorite spices

- Heat palm oil in a heavy frying pan

- Begin frying fish 2 or 3 pieces at a time

- Turn it every few minutes until it is cooked

- Remove it and place it over a plate or basket

Continue the frying activities until completion

N.B. *Fried fish can be served with – Rice, fried plantain, fried yam or mashed plantain or mashed yam.*

YAMS

In the Congo RDC there are four types of Yams. They can be distinguished from their colors. The first type is white inside, the second type is pinkish, and the third type is golden inside. The fourth type however grows wild in the forest it appears white inside, whereas the other kinds of yams can be cultivated.

All kinds of yams can be fried in palm oil, peanut oil or any other types of oils preferred.

Yams can be boiled just like potatoes. Yams can also be smashed. This option depends on personal taste or preference.

RECIPES - MBALA YA KOKALINGA (Fried Yam)

Ingredients

1-2 lbs peeled yams

Frying pan

2 cups palm oil

Preparation

- *Wash yams thoroughly*
- *Peel skins carefully*
- *Slice yams in regular pieces*
- *Heat oil in the frying pan*
- Wait for about 5 minutes
- Begin to fry few pieces at a time.
- Make sure to turn the pieces back and forth to prevent burning.
- Remove the golden pieces or which are already cooked.

- Place them in a nice clean plate or a bowl.
- Cover the bowl in order to keep them warm.
- Replace new pieces in the frying pan and repeat the process until finish.

Ready to be served with any main dishes – Meat, fish, Shrimps or vegetables.

PLANTAIN RECIPES

There are three types of plantain recipes in the Congo RDC. It all depends on the types of texture.

The yellow plantain can be prepared in three different recipes:

1. Fried
2. Boil
3. Smashed

GREEN PLANTAIN

The green plantains can be prepared in two different recipes:

1. Fried

2. Boil

RECIPES - FRIED YELLOW PLANTAIN
MAKEMBA YA KOKALINGA (Fried Plantains)

Ingredients

4 peeled Plantains

Cutting board and knife

Frying pan

cups palm oil

Preparation

- *Wash plantains thoroughly*
- *Peel skins carefully*
- *Slice plantains in regular pieces*
- *or just cut normal pieces.*
- *Heat oil in the frying pan*
- Wait for about 5 minutes
- Begin to fry few pieces at a time.
- Make sure to turn the pieces back and forth to prevent burning.
- Remove the golden pieces or which are already cooked.
- Place them in a nice clean plate or a bowl.
- Cover the bowl in order to keep them warm.
- Replace new pieces in the frying pan and repeat the process until finish.

N.B. Ready to be served with any main dish – Meat, fish, chicken, duck, shrimps or vegetables.

Green Plantains

Fried - Recipes

Ingredients

3 peels green plantains

Cutting board and knife

Frying pan

1 ½ cup of palm oil/ or any other

Preparation

- Wash green plantains
- Peel of the skins
- Place on the cutting board
- Cut into regular pieces or into slice.
- Heat the oil in the frying pan
- Begin frying few pieces at the time.

- Remove when cooked and place them in the plate and cover the lid in order to keep them warm.
- Replace new pieces in the frying pan and repeat the process until finish.

N.B. ***Ready to be served with any main dish – Meat, fish, chicken, duck, shrimps or vegetables***.

MIKATE (TRADITIONAL Doughnuts

MIKATE YA LOSO NA TANGAWISI (Rice donuts in Ginger liquid)

Ingredients

- 2 lbs of rice flour/or all purpose flour
- ½ fresh ginger liquid
- 1pt of water
- 2 cups of sugar
- 1/2 teaspoon salt
- ½ teaspoon yeast
- 1 pt of palm oil/or any other

Preparation

- In a big mixing bowl, place rice flour
- Add water and mix it thoroughly
- Add ginger liquid and stir completely
- Add yeast, stir for about 2 minutes
- Stir ingredients vigorously
- Add salt in the dough, and mix everything together
- Beat until all the ingredients are combined smoothly.
- On a heavy frying pan or skillet, heat 1 pt of palm oil
- Begin taking a small amount of dough
- Deep it in hot oil until the dough changes from white to brownish color.

- Remove the well done Mikate and place them in the basket to let the oil drip, and then remove them and place them in a clean big plate.
- Continue the operation until the frying activity has been completed.

N.B. ***Mikate can be served hot or cool***. People usually eat mikate for breakfast, with coffee or herb teas. Some people can eat mikate for snacks, whereas others would eat it after a meal as a dessert. It all depends upon individuals' taste and preference. There is no set rule to this.

MEAT STEW (RECIPES)

Ingredients

2-3lbs of meat

½ cup of palm oil

5cups of water

3 medium ripe tomatoes

1/2 canned tomatoes

Spices – Bay leave, celery, hot pepper (or onion, etc.

PREPARATION

- *Clean meat*
- *Put in a heavy cooking pot*
- *Season it*
- *Parboil for about 1 hour*
- *Remove from the heat*
- *Heat palm oil in a frying pan*
- *Wait until the oil turns orange color*

- *Fry meat until it turns golden*
- *Remove from the frying pan*
- *Place it in a heavy cooking pot*
- *Add the remaining water from the initial pot*
- *Heat new fresh oil in a frying pan*
- *Wait until it turns golden*
- *Add chopped tomatoes and ½ canned tomatoes and spices.*
- *Let it cook until for 5 minutes*
- *Pour in the pot*
- *Cover it and let it cook for 35 minutes*
- *Use your discretion if the duck is not well cooked*
- *Add some more water-*
- *Let it cook for about fifteen minutes*
- *Reduce the heat and let it simmer*
- *Remove from the heat*

   Ready to serve- With either, rice, chikwangue, plantain, fufu, couscous, Sweet potatoes or Yam.

N.B. The meat recipes various with individual taste, it can be baked, fried, or cooked in tomatoes sauce.

THE FOLLOWING SECTION DEPICTS PICTURES OF SOME DISHES AND FEW IMAGES OF RAW CONGOLESE VEGETABLES.

PONDU VEGETABLE (is also called Saka-Saka in Kikongo ya L'Etat, or Feuilles de Manioc in French (Cassava Leaves in English)

PONDU is a Congolese National Vegetable Dish

Organically cultivated vegetable

Cooked RegularPondu

With green and red pepper in palm oil

Pondu ya kolamba na poivrons

NA MAFUTA YA MBILA

Cooked Limbondo Pondu

Green Pondu with Sardine

Pondu ya limbondo na Sardine

Frozen Pondu Cooked with Egg plant

Pondu vegetable can be cooked with egg plant or green squash

Mixed with green pepper and red pepper.

SEEDS RECIPES

RAW PAMPKIN SEEDS (Green seed)

M B I KA YA MOBESO

NTERE

MANTETE

Pumpkin Seed Baked traditionally

The dough is wrapped in Nzombi leaves (Makasa ya Nzombi/kwanga)

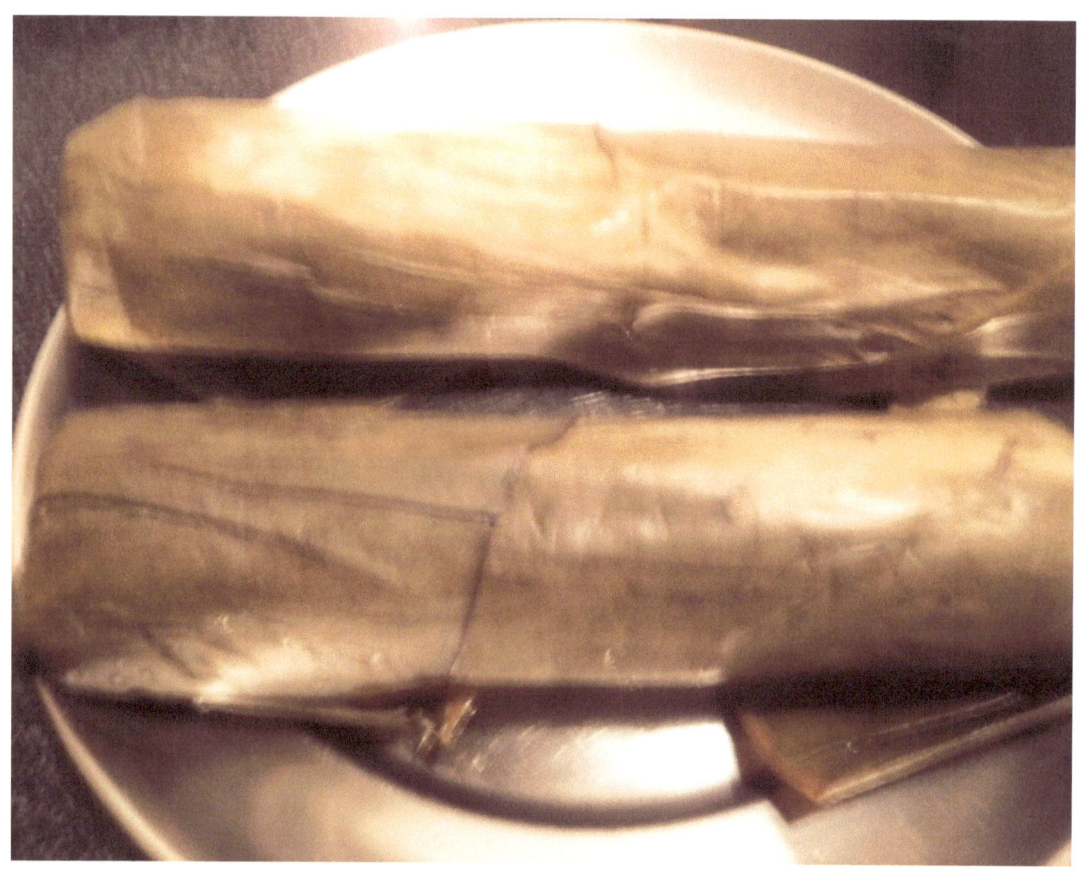

Pumpkin seeds baked traditionally in zombie leaves.

BAKED PUMPKIN SEED

With Mushroom

Baked from baking pan

Baked pumpkin seed with mushrooms and traditional spices.

CREVETES NA MBIKA (NTERE, MANTETE)

SHRIMPS IN MPUMPKIN SEED SAUCE

SHRIMPS IN PUMPKIN SAUCE

FRIED SHRIMPS IN PALM OIL

CREVETES YA KOKALINGA NA MAFUTA YA MBILA

DONGO-DONGO RECIPES

Whole OKRA

Dongo-Dongo ya Mobeso

DONGO-DONGO YA MOBESA RAW CUT OKRAS

Dongo-Dongo ya Mobeso Raw OKRAS

Cooked Okras with Mushroom and Green Paper
Vegetarian style

Dongo-Dongo na Mayebo/Poivrons

Okra can be cooked with sea food (shrimps, baby shrimps, dried/smoked fish, crabs, makayabo (cat fish), mushroom or just plain.

MADESO YA BA SODA NA MAFUTA YA MBILA

KIDNEY BEANS COOKED IN PALM OIL

FRIED WHITE YAM

MBALA YA KOTOKISA (BOILED YAM)

BOILED WHITE YAM

Matuluku = Yuca

Unpeeled Yuca

Matuluku is cooked by boiling it after you have peeled it, and then, cut it in medium nice sizes. Boiled it until it is soft enough to eat.

CHIKWANGA OR KWANGA

UNWRAPED CHIKWANGA

CHIKWANGA COUPE (CUT CHIKWANGA)
Bi teni ya Kwanga

FUFU

Good nutritious fufu is made out of ½ amount of cassava flour and ½ amount of Corn meal (flour) in boiling water. It yields golden color.

Fufu ya Masango

PLANTAIN

Yellow plantains can be boiled

Can be mashed when they are well ripped can be fried.

MASHED PLANTAIN

Some parts of the country prefer to eat mashed plantain with fish

MIKATE (Traditional doughnut)

Mikate (traditional doughnut) can be made in various tastes and formats. It all depends upon individuals' preference. It can be made with all purpose flour or with rice flour and spices.

It can be made plain; regular or the maker can add some spices to give it an exotic taste. Therefore mikate doughnut may also vary in the appearance and format.

Mikate ya loso/to ya farine

MBISI YA KOKALINGA — FRIED FISH

Bimbata (tilapia) or many other different types of fishes can be fried or can be cooked in tomatoes sauce

BIMBATA (TILAPIA) FISH

Tilapia fish is the most popular fish grown in the Bantu peoples' ponds of the Congo RDC besides from many other types.

BILOLO VEGETABLE

Bilolo vegetable can be steamed or they can be mixed with other ingredients.

VEGETARIAN STYLE

BILOLO VEGETABLE

BILOLO VEGETABLE CAN BE STEAMED

It can also be cooked with mushroom, green or red pepper. It can be cooked with boneless dried or smoked fish, or with makayabo (cat fish) – It all depends on preference.

Biteko-teko (Kalaloo) Vegetable

Biteko-teko (Kalaloo) Vegetable

Biteko-teko (Kalaloo) Vegetable can be cooked in combination with green, red pepper, and fresh tomatoes, it can be served with Plantain (boiled, fried or smashed). It depends on individuals' preference.

Matembele Vegetable

Matembele vegetable is one of the preferred vegetables in the Bantu society of the Congo RDC. Like the other Congolese vegetable. Matembele Vegetable is organically grown.

Matembele organic vegetable

POULET A LA MWAMBA
CHICKEN IN PEANUT BUTTER SAUCE

CHICKEN COOKED IN PALM OIL

FRESH TOMATOES

PEANUT BUTTER

AND SPICES

A FULL MEAL
CHICKEN, PONDU AND RICE

- Chicken can be prepared following different recipes:
- Chicken in peanut butter sauce
- Chicken in pumpkin sauce
- Chicken in tomatoes sauce

or fried chicken - It all depends on individuals' preferences.

BEPONA BOOKS

Africa Presents

- The Congo RDC and Lingala Language (English and French version (First edition) - **LINGALA DICTIONARY - by Bopona Collection**

- The Congo RDC and Kikongo Language (English and French version (first edition). - **KIKONGO ya L'Etat DICTIONARY - by Bepona Collection**

- The Congo RDC and Child Education (First edition)

- The Congo RDC and Congolese Cuisine (First edition)

- The Congo RDC and A Congolese Woman Chief (Mfumu-Mkento)

- The Congo RDC Et la Femme Congolese Dirigeante (Mfumu-Nkento)

- The Congo RDC and Tradition Law (first edition)

- The Congo RDC and Congolese Comedy/Novel

    1. A Mysterious Boy called Timo Mikwaya Well known as Kamina

    2. Mr. Aleyi-Atondi

    How can this man live with his In-laws for over 15 years?

    3. A Western Professor with an African University Student (Abelengezi)

    4. Experience of two African young ladies in America (Magoke)

By

Bepona Collection

ABOUT BEPONA COLLECTION

Our books are written by Americans of African descent, particularly from the Congo RDC (located in Central Africa) – *MPA, PAS, BBA, and BA*. The Congolese society is composed of the Bantu Peoples and the Pygmies. These American authors of the African descent have been compelled to share the Congolese culture with those individuals who are interested in diversity.

Our educational books are factual. They are based on our own personal research which we had conducted scholarly, and confirmed by the oral traditions of the Bantu peoples, which were transmitted to us by our live Historians. The live historians are actually the wise living senior citizens who continue to maintain and sustain the authenticity of the oral traditions without distortion

Generally, Bepona Collection's books are apolitical. We concentrate our books on presenting the Congolese culture, which encompasses general social issues. Evidently, our contemporary history is connected to our ancient traditions. And therefore, we cannot omit touching some other topics, although slightly- sometimes-when we write about the Congolese culture.

Our novels are practically, narrative non-fiction. The names of the characters including the original setting have been withheld intentionally, in order to protect the privacy or identities of the individuals concerned.

All our books are written in simple terms, language and style. Our goal is to share our culture and to express ourselves, but not to impress our readers.

KINSHASA, THE CAPITAL CITY OF THE Congo RDC PRIOR TO THE CIVIL WAR

DEMOCRATIC REPUBLIC OF CONGO

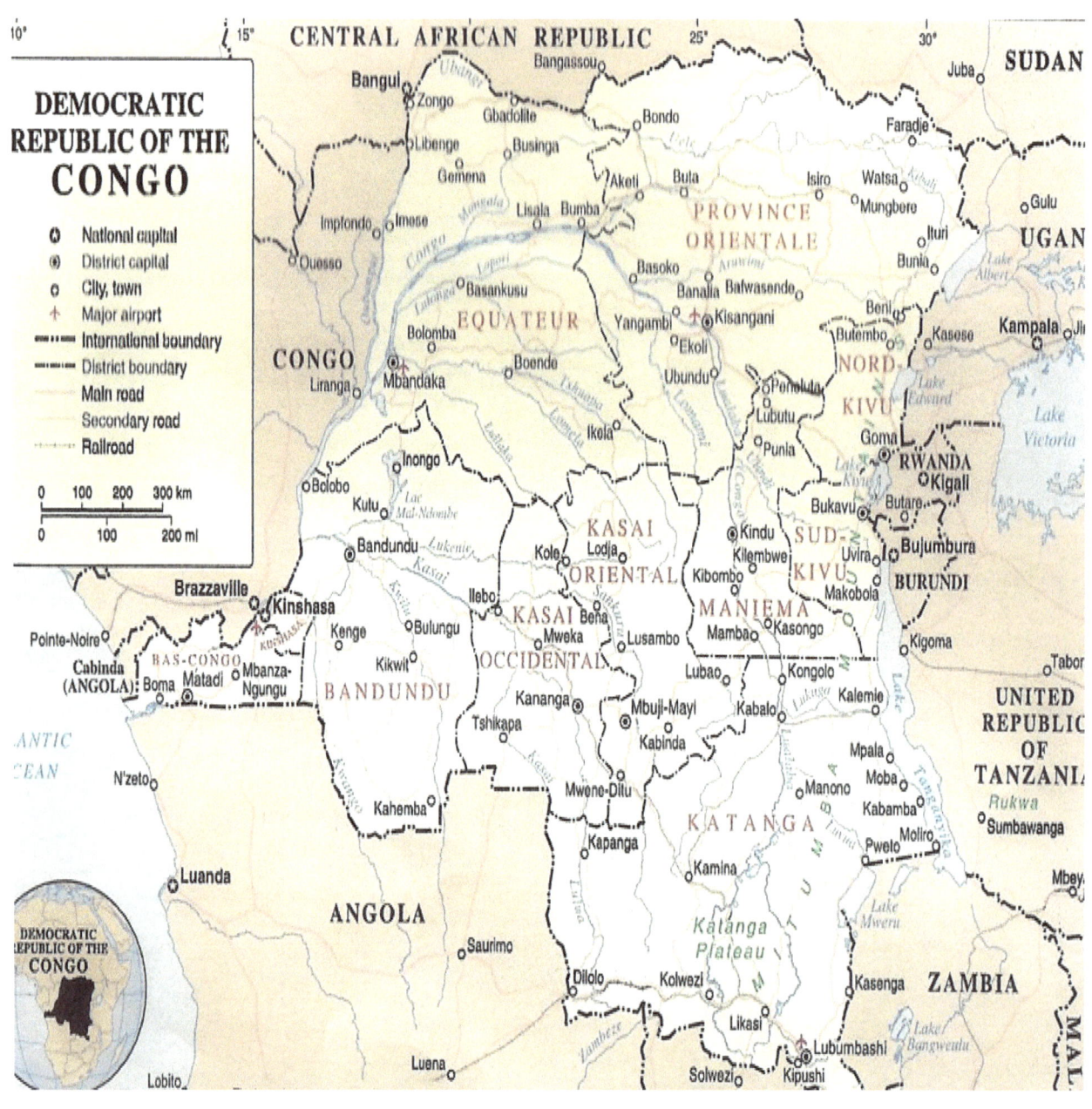

AFRICA

www.ingramcontent.com/pod-product-compliance
Ingram Content Group UK Ltd.
Pitfield, Milton Keynes, MK11 3LW, UK
UKHW060137240426

12048UKWH00002B/83